W9-CDM-953

Understanding the Coronavirus

The Future
of Coronavirus

Margaret J. Goldstein

Lerner Publications ◆ Minneapolis

Lerner Publications Company
An imprint of Lerner Publishing Group, Inc.
241 First Avenue North
Minneapolis, MN 55401 USA

For reading levels and more information, look up this title at www.lernerbooks.com.

Main body text set in Adrianna Regular.
Typeface provided by Chank.

Library of Congress Cataloging-in-Publication Data

Names: Goldstein, Margaret J., author.
Title: The future of coronavirus / Margaret J. Goldstein.
Description: Minneapolis : Lerner Publications , [2022] | Series: Searchlight books - understanding the coronavirus | Includes bibliographical references and index. | Audience: Ages 8–11 | Audience: Grades 4–6 | Summary: "Deadly coronavirus diseases such as COVID-19 can disrupt societies. Find out how health-care professionals will fight these viruses in the future with vaccines, preventative measures, and therapeutics"— Provided by publisher.
Identifiers: LCCN 2021003217 (print) | LCCN 2021003218 (ebook) | ISBN 9781728428482 (library binding) | ISBN 9781728431451 (paperback) | ISBN 9781728430737 (ebook)
Subjects: LCSH: COVID-19 (Disease)—Juvenile literature. | COVID-19 (Disease)—Social aspects—Juvenile literature. | COVID-19 (Disease)—Treatment—Juvenile literature. | COVID-19 (Disease)—Prevention—Juvenile literature.
Classification: LCC RA644.C67 G646 2022 (print) | LCC RA644.C67 (ebook) | DDC 362.1962/414—dc23

LC record available at https://lccn.loc.gov/2021003217
LC ebook record available at https://lccn.loc.gov/2021003218

Manufactured in the United States of America
1-49385-49489-4/26/2021

Table of Contents

Chapter 1

A TOUGH 2020

The year 2020 presented the challenge of a lifetime. A virus called SARS-CoV-2, a new coronavirus, spread around the world. The virus made people sick with coughs, fevers, and body aches. The disease caused by the virus was named COVID-19. Some people with COVID-19 had trouble breathing. While most patients recovered at home, many needed hospital care. Some patients died.

The virus spread from person to person. To keep workers from infecting one another, many offices closed. Employees worked from home instead. Schools operated online too. In many places, restaurants, stores, movie theaters, and sports stadiums shut down. Customers ordered food and other goods online for home delivery. Friends socialized from home using video chat. When people left their houses, they wore face masks to keep the virus from passing from person to person.

People protect themselves and others by wearing masks in public places.

In memory of the 200,000+ Americans who have needlessly lost their lives to COVID-19

#COVIDMemo oject

Flags are placed in a cemetery in late September 2020 to represent the number of American lives lost to COVID-19.

Even with masks and social distancing, millions of people got sick with COVID-19. Around the world, hospitals were swamped with patients. Doctors and nurses struggled to take care of everyone. By April 2021, more than 120 million people had been infected and nearly 3 million had died.

Dr. Katalin Karikó

Dr. Katalin Karikó (*below*) grew up in Hungary in central Europe. She studied biochemistry in college. Karikó moved to the United States in 1985 to work as a professor and medical researcher. As part of this work, she studied messenger RNA (mRNA), a type of molecule inside cells. She figured out how to use mRNA to make a new type of vaccine. Drug companies used her technique to make the COVID-19 vaccine. They will use it to make vaccines for other diseases in the future.

Turning the Corner on COVID-19

Medical researchers developed vaccines to protect people from the virus. Vaccination began in late 2020. The goal was to vaccinate most people on Earth. That would limit the spread of the virus or even stop it altogether.

What will happen when the pandemic is over? Will life go back to normal? No one knows for sure. But some changes brought by COVID-19 will probably remain, even when the virus is gone.

Health workers vaccinate millions of people every week.

Chapter 2

THE HOME FRONT

As COVID-19 spread around the world, people shopped online because it was safer than shopping in stores. Supermarkets and other stores offered curbside pickup and home delivery. After the pandemic, stores will be safe again. But most people will still do some online shopping because it's fast and easy.

Zoom, Microsoft Teams, and Google Meet are some of the platforms used to help people have meetings and class sessions from home.

Many office workers stayed home during the pandemic. They worked from home computers. Many workers liked this new system. They didn't need to travel to and from work by car, bus, or subway. That saved lots of time. Businesses also benefited. With workers at home, companies didn't need to spend money on big offices. Numerous business leaders say that when the pandemic ends, they will still let employees work from home.

Working from home was not an option for everyone. Grocery workers, farmworkers, delivery drivers, hospital workers, and many others can't do their jobs online. These essential workers traveled to and from their workplaces despite the risk of COVID-19. They will continue to do their jobs in person when the pandemic is over.

Grocery workers protect themselves and others from the virus by wearing masks, face shields, and gloves.

STUDENTS OFTEN USE COMPUTERS OR TABLETS WHEN DOING SCHOOLWORK FROM HOME.

The New School

To keep students, teachers, and other school staff safe from infection, many schools switched to online learning. Students with home computers accessed online videos, e-books, lessons, lectures, and tests. Students had video chats with teachers. However, some students didn't have home computers or reliable internet access. They missed out on lessons.

When the pandemic ends, the majority of students will return to their classrooms. Most students do their best work when they have in-person interactions with classmates and teachers. But online learning won't go away. Schools might combine in-classroom and at-home learning. One challenge will be making sure that all students have home computers and fast, reliable internet access for online learning.

Wearing masks and spacing desks at least 6 feet (2 m) apart are two ways students and educators try to keep people safe in schools.

Cities after COVID-19

Cities changed when COVID-19 arrived. To avoid crowds, some people moved from cities to small towns or suburbs. With the shift to online shopping, a lot of retailers shut down their storefronts. Some restaurants went out of business. Many offices sat empty because staff members worked from home. Museums, concert halls, and sports arenas shut down too.

After the pandemic, cities will come back to life. People love dining out and watching live sports and entertainment. But if people continue to work and shop from home, some offices and stores might not reopen. Some government leaders suggest new uses for these spaces. In many cities, housing is in short supply. Builders might turn the empty stores and offices into affordable homes for city residents.

Sorry We're
CLOSED
Due to COVID 19

State and local governments provide guidelines for when businesses need to close due to COVID-19.

Laurie Garrett

In the 1990s, science journalist Laurie Garrett (*below*) predicted the future. She noted that Earth's human population was growing quickly. Many people lived in crowded cities. Travelers could fly from country to country in just a few hours. Lots of people in contact with one another made it easier for infectious diseases to spread. In her 1994 book *The Coming Plague*, Garrett predicted future pandemics. Many of her predictions came true during the COVID-19 pandemic.

Chapter 3

PANDEMIC TECHNOLOGY

Public health experts told people to stand at least 6 feet (2 m) away from others to prevent COVID-19 infection. That wasn't easy. At many workplaces, employees interacted closely with one another and with customers. Many of them got sick with COVID-19.

A ROOM SERVICE ROBOT DELIVERS FOOD TO HOTEL GUESTS.

▼

Some businesses solved this problem with robots. One fast-food chain replaced human kitchen workers with robotic cooking machines. They grilled hamburgers and fried potatoes and other foods. A hotel chain used robots to deliver towels and meals to guests. Some companies used small drones to deliver products to online shoppers.

Cleaning robots also helped businesses. Cleaning regularly helps reduce the spread of COVID-19 since the virus can live on furniture, smartphones, and other objects. The machines used ultraviolet light to kill germs in hospital rooms, airplanes, and other spaces.

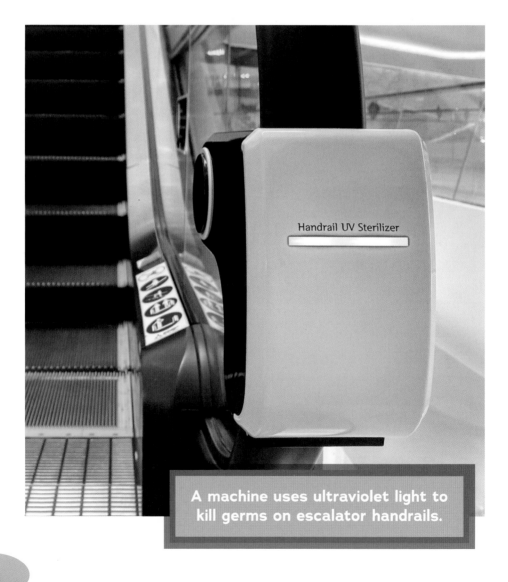

Handrail UV Sterilizer

A machine uses ultraviolet light to kill germs on escalator handrails.

On delivery

When the pandemic is over, businesses will keep using robots. They perform tasks over and over again without getting tired or making mistakes. But robots have downsides. They can't think and make decisions like human workers. They can also lead to unemployment when they take over people's jobs.

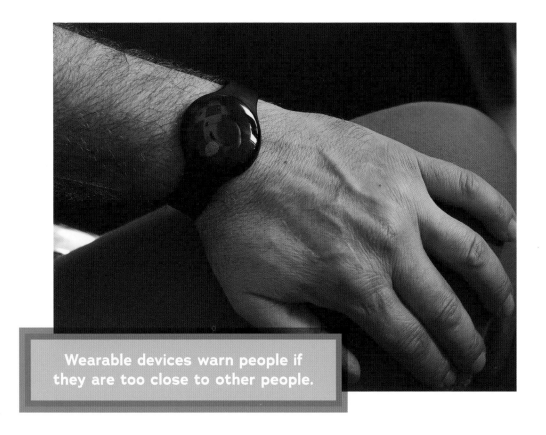

Wearable devices warn people if they are too close to other people.

Gearheads

Inventors got busy during the pandemic. They built gadgets to help people cope with COVID-19. One is a wristband that tracks the wearer's distance from others. It flashes a warning light if two people stand less than 6 feet (2 m) apart. Another wearable device takes the person's temperature throughout the day. If the wearer develops a fever, one symptom of COVID-19, the device sounds an alert.

STEM Spotlight

To prevent the spread of the coronavirus, public health experts told people to wash their hands often. Doing so removes virus particles from the skin. Another way to keep hands virus-free is to avoid touching surfaces. Even before the pandemic, touchless technology was common. Examples include motion-activated faucets, voice-activated digital assistants, and smartphone payment readers. The pandemic made touchless technology more popular. Touch-free thermometers are one example. Nurses use them to detect people with fevers from a safe distance.

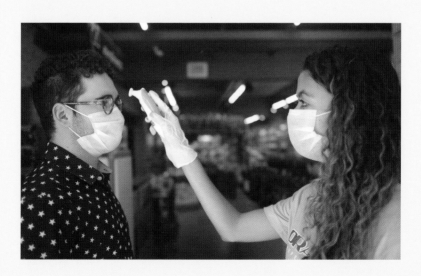

Most people wore simple cloth face masks during the pandemic. But one company built a smart face mask. The plastic mask has a speaker to make the wearer's voice louder. It can even translate speech into eight different languages.

The new technology is probably here to stay. For instance, distance trackers will remind people to practice social distancing during future virus outbreaks. Drones and robots can help keep people virus-free and streamline business operations. They will surely be part of our post-pandemic future.

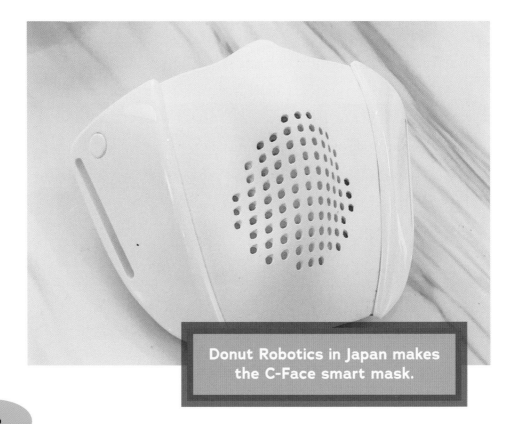

Donut Robotics in Japan makes the C-Face smart mask.

Chapter 4

HEALTH CARE REVOLUTION

In hospitals and clinics, the coronavirus spread from patient to patient. It also spread from patients to doctors and nurses. To block the virus, health workers wore face masks, face shields, and plastic gowns. Health leaders let only patients requiring serious medical attention into hospitals and medical offices. Other patients stayed home and talked to their doctors on video chats.

Doctors monitored some patients remotely. New technology made it easier. Some patients wore watches or wristbands that tracked their heart rate, pulse, and blood pressure. The devices sent that data to doctors over wireless networks. Doctors used the data to figure out what treatment patients needed. Patients could stay safe at home but still get medical care.

Doctors use data from smart watches to monitor their patients.

TELEMEDICINE ALLOWS PATIENTS TO STILL MEET WITH DOCTORS AND NURSES.

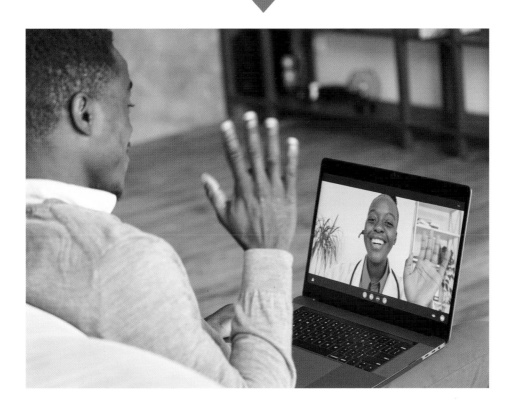

Telemedicine isn't perfect. Sometimes, doctors need to examine a patient in person to treat an illness. When the pandemic is over, patients will return to doctors' offices. But doctors will still use telemedicine and remote monitoring to gather information. Then they will decide if an in-person visit is needed.

STEM Spotlight

Doctors and nurses weren't the only ones who helped patients during the pandemic. Medical chatbots helped too. These smartphone apps asked patients about their symptoms and health histories. If a bot determined that a person might have COVID-19, it suggested a COVID-19 test or a trip to the emergency room. Medical chatbots use artificial intelligence to discuss health care with patients. They are likely to become more common after the pandemic.

Acting Fast

When the pandemic hit, vaccine researchers went into high gear. It usually takes several years to make a vaccine. But with millions of people getting sick and dying of COVID-19, researchers had no time to waste. They worked hard. The COVID-19 vaccine was ready in less than a year.

To treat COVID-19 patients, scientists developed new medicines. But they were frustrated. Many of the new drugs were ineffective. Even so, the research was important. It helped researchers better understand COVID-19.

Universities and companies continue to research and test new vaccines.

Wearing masks and social distancing in public help people stay safe from the coronavirus.

What Lies Ahead?

Even after the pandemic, COVID-19 might not disappear completely. To protect themselves from the coronavirus, people might need a COVID-19 vaccine every year. New diseases might spread as well. But the world will be better prepared next time. Scientists and governments will know how to slow infection rates using social distancing and face masks. Medical researchers will know how to make vaccines and drugs quickly. The lessons of the coronavirus will guide us to a healthier future.

Important Dates

December 2019   Government officials in China report a new virus outbreak in the city of Wuhan.

January 2020   Health officials report the first COVID-19 case in the United States.

March 2020   The World Health Organization declares the coronavirus outbreaks to be a pandemic.

April 2020   The Centers for Disease Control and Prevention (CDC) advises everyone to wear face masks when in public.

May 2020   The US government announces Operation Warp Speed, a project to produce and distribute a COVID-19 vaccine in record time.

November 2020   Three drug companies announce that they have developed effective COVID-19 vaccines.

December 2020   US health workers begin receiving COVID-19 vaccines.

Glossary

artificial intelligence: technology that imitates human thought and communication

coronavirus: a virus whose surface is covered by spiky projections

drone: an aircraft that can fly without a pilot and is guided by remote control

essential worker: a person whose work is needed to keep society running

infectious disease: a sickness that occurs when a germ or other substance enters the body and reproduces itself

molecule: the smallest possible amount of a substance that has all the characteristics of that substance

pandemic: a worldwide outbreak of a disease

social distancing: keeping a certain amount of space between yourself and others, usually 6 feet (2 m), to prevent the spread of disease from person to person

telemedicine: a doctor visit conducted over the internet rather than in person

vaccine: a substance that prepares the immune system to fight off an invader, such as a virus

virus: a tiny particle that can infect living cells and cause disease

Learn More

Biology for Kids: Viruses
    https://www.ducksters.com/science/biology/viruses.php

Coronavirus: What Kids Can Do
    https://kidshealth.org/en/kids/coronavirus-kids.html

Gilles, Renae. *The Science of Coronavirus*. Minneapolis: Lerner
    Publications, 2020.

Macgregor, Eloise. *Be a Virus Warrior! A Kid's Guide to Keeping Safe*.
    New York: Rosen, 2020.

Race to a Vaccine
    https://www.timeforkids.com/g56/race-to-a-vaccine-2/?rl=en-880

Slade, Suzanne. *June Almeida, Virus Detective!: The Woman Who
    Discovered the First Human Coronavirus*. Ann Arbor, MI: Sleeping
    Bear Press, 2021.

Index

Photo Acknowledgments

Image credits: FamVeld/Shutterstock, p.5; TJ Brown/Shutterstock, p.6; Krdobyns/Wikimedia, p.7; Prostock-studio/Shutterstock, p.8; Andrey_Popov/ZUMA Wire/Shutterstock, p.10; Tempura/Getty Images, p.11; Mayur Kakade/Getty Images, p.12; izusek/Getty Images, p.13; Kanawa_Studio/Daily Express/Hulton Archive/Getty Images, p.14; Michael Loccisano/Getty Images, p.15; ZUMA Press/Cover Images/Philadelphia Inquirer/MCT/Newscom, p.17; happycreator/Atlanta Journal-Constitution/TNS/Shutterstock, p.18; Austin Nooe/Shutterstock, p.19; Carlos Alvarez/Getty Images, p.20; Andre Coelho/Stringer/ZUMA Wire/Getty Images, p.21; Donut Robotics/Cover Images/Newscom, p.22; DenPhotos/Shutterstock, p.24; insta_photos/Shutterstock, p.25; Tero Vesalainen/Shutterstock, p.26; Karen Ducey/rosiekeystrokes/Getty Images, p.27; Travelpixs/Shutterstock, p.28

Cover: Kiyoshi Hijiki/Getty Images